> ## "When the economy changes ... I'm outta' here!"
>
> ## "Is it 5:00 yet?"
>
> ## "Why bother... management doesn't care what we think."

The research is very clear. Around the world, employee engagement is on the decline.[1] In the United States alone, the lost productivity of actively disengaged employees costs the economy $370 billion annually.[2] That is a very scary number!

Regardless of our job titles or positions, every one of us can make a positive impact on engagement – changes that affect ourselves, those we lead, and our peers. To do this, we need to take advantage of the most important skill set we have: our communication skills.

This little book packs a big punch when it comes to developing remarkable communication skills that will enhance employee engagement. With a focus on practical application, language patterns, and specific "words to choose" and "words to lose," this book is jam-packed with communication tools you can put to use immediately.

Communicate To Keep 'Em
Enhancing Employee Engagement
Through Remarkable Communication

ISBN 978-1-939614-12-4

Communicate

To Keep 'Em

Enhancing employee engagement
through remarkable communication

Pamela Jett

*Courage is what it takes
to stand up and speak;
courage is also what it takes
to sit down and listen.*

~ Winston Churchill

TABLE OF CONTENTS

Introduction . . . . **vii**

Chapter 1 Employee Engagement, Communication, and Golf 1

Chapter 2 Choose Your Mindset 3

Chapter 3 Change "Will this work?" to "How will this work?" 5

Chapter 4 Words Matter! The Case of "That" vs. "If" 9

Chapter 5 Practice Assertive Communication 15

Chapter 6 Right vs. Effective **19**

Chapter 7 Sorry No More! **23**

Chapter 8 Communicate in the Positive **25**

Chapter 9 Ditch the "Don't" and Focus on
the Desired Behavior **29**

Chapter 10 Forget Forgetting **31**

Chapter 11 Communicating: "Power To" vs. "Power Over" **33**

Chapter 12 Ask Open-Ended Questions **37**

Chapter 13 That's Interesting, Tell Me More **41**

Chapter 14 Does Anyone Have Any Questions? **45**

Chapter 15 Like Best/Next Time **47**

Chapter 16 Beware the "But" **57**

Chapter 17 "Are you open to some feedback?" **59**

Chapter 18 Express Appreciation **61**

Chapter 19 Please **65**

Chapter 20 The Art of Praising **69**

Chapter 21 Practice Straight Line Communication **73**

Chapter 22 In Absence of Good Information... . . . .**75**

Chapter 23 A Few Habits to Break **77**

Chapter 24 Now What? **83**

Endnotes **85**

About Pamela Jett **87**

*Communication is like a thread
which runs through a pearl necklace.
It is invisible.
Yet without it,
everything would fall apart.*

~ Pamela Jett

INTRODUCTION

Why All the Fuss About Employee Engagement?

Definitions of employee engagement abound. This is the one I like the best:

> **Engagement is the willingness and ability to contribute to company success – the extent to which employees put discretionary effort into their work in the form of extra time, brainpower, and energy.** [3]

Employees who are engaged are emotionally committed to their work and to their organizations. Engaged employees show up to work and give their best. They offer up new ideas and suggestions. They are positive and energized. They are interested in their organizations' success. Engaged employees display an "I care" attitude.

Disengaged employees are not emotionally committed to their work and their organizations. They show up to work, but only do the minimum amount required. They typically don't make suggestions, offer up new ideas, or in any way do more than what is required to collect their paychecks. The disengaged employee will often display an "Is it Friday yet?" attitude. They strongly resist change, and rarely, if ever, offer suggestions or ideas for improvement.

As a result, innovation and productivity both suffer. Absenteeism abounds, and when the disengaged do show up, they spend their time thinking about when they can quit and find a better job someplace else. And what if they stay? In that case, the disengaged employee can make their co-workers miserable.

Just how pervasive a problem is disengagement? It's a problem that cuts across global boundaries, job types, and industries.[4] Research reveals that barely 1 in 5 employees are engaged on the job and the rest fall into some category of disengagement.[5]

In general, there are two broad types of disengaged employees: the actively disengaged and the passively disengaged.

The actively disengaged, which comprise about 8 percent of the workforce, can be understood as the gossips, the whiners, and the overtly resistant to change. They are the employees who will deny responsibility for setbacks or challenges, often blaming them on other teams or departments or on organizational policies. They project a negative attitude about everyone and everything. Worse yet, because misery loves company, they often try to undermine the success of others or attempt to bring others onto their negativity bandwagon.

Although actively disengaged workers make up less than 10% of the workforce, they are toxic, and capable of doing tremendous damage. When I work with leaders in my live workshops, I often ask them how much of their time, effort, and energy as leaders is put into managing this "bottom 10%" and undoing the havoc they create. The answer is uniformly, "Far too much!"

While not as overtly negative and destructive as the actively disengaged, the passively disengaged aren't really happy at work. Outside the workplace, they aren't advocates for their company or its products and services. Worse yet, they don't fully understand the impact their actions have on organizational goals and objectives. This is often a result of leaders not engaging in clear communication that fosters trust, open dialogue, and other drivers of innovation and productivity.

Enhancing employee engagement can yield tremendous and measurable business benefits. Consider:

- Higher levels of engagement are strongly related to higher levels of innovation.[6]

- High engagement correlates strongly with measurable improved organizational performance in key areas such as shareholder return and annual net income.[7]

- Engaged employees stay at their organizations, reducing the high cost of turnover.[8]

Given the tremendous benefits of an engaged workforce and the high cost of disengagement ($370 billion annually due to lost productivity in the U.S. alone), improving employee engagement ought to be a top priority for leaders at every level. It is also the responsibility of every employee to enhance their own engagement as well as that of their peers.

The great news is that the way you communicate with those you lead and those you work with (and even how you communicate with yourself) can have a tremendous impact on employee engagement, especially on those who are passively disengaged. Communication significantly impacts many of the major drivers of employee engagement, such as:

- The quality of working relationships with leaders, subordinates, and peers

- Clarity of job expectations and importance

- Trust in leadership

- Feedback

- Conversations about career advancement/opportunity

If you communicate in a manner that conveys respect and avoids the words and phrases that trigger defensiveness and animosity, you can do your part to enhance employee engagement within your own sphere of influence. If you communicate in a way that is clear and confident, you inspire trust and encourage dialogue.

Obviously, enhancing employee engagement on a company-wide level is more than a one-person job. Employee engagement is a complicated issue that requires effort at all levels of the organization. Upper management in particular must buy into the importance of engagement and enact an appropriate engagement-boosting strategy within the workplace.

However, any large employee engagement initiative is doomed to fail if individual managers, leaders, and influential employees are not doing their part in day-to-day communication and interaction.

That is where this book comes in. It is loaded with practical communication tools, tips, and techniques you can begin to use today to do your part to enhance employee engagement. These powerful tools are grounded in real-world application and have been used by thousands worldwide. The remarkable communication tools in this book will enable you to begin to enhance employee engagement within your sphere of influence, and your team and colleagues will reap the rewards.

Choose to be, as Tom Peters would say, an "island of excellence."[9] Regardless of what upper management does or does not do to promote employee engagement, regardless of how our fellow leaders choose to think and behave, and regardless of how our peers choose to function, each one of us can make a personal commitment to be an island of excellence even if we are floating in a sea of mediocrity.

Choose to do your part to create an engaged culture. Choose to be the type of leader your employees want to work with and for. Choose to engage in positive behaviors that convey respect. Imagine what your workplace or your team could be like if you choose to use engaging communication. Your team would be a happier, more collaborative, more innovative group. Do your part to make that a reality. And who knows? You just might engage others in your efforts and your island of excellence will grow.

Each tool in this book is a stand-alone technique you can put to work immediately. This means you can read through page by page or just jump in anywhere. Enjoy!

   - Pamela Jett

CHAPTER 1

Employee Engagement, Communication, and Golf

Communication is a bit like professional golf. If you've ever watched a golf tournament, you've likely noticed that the person who comes in first and the person who comes in second are only separated by a few swings or strokes of the golf club – sometimes as few as one or two.

In terms of prize money, however, as little as one swing of the golf club can make all the difference!

As with golf, small changes in how we communicate can have a huge impact on employee engagement. Making a conscious effort to choose our words wisely, use techniques that build relationships, and use language that builds people up as opposed to tearing them down can make all the difference with respect to building good working relationships. This is crucial because positive relationships are one of the key drivers of employee engagement.

If we practice better communication, we will have better relationships, more engaged employees, stronger bonds with our families, enhanced workplace productivity, and a reputation as the kind of person others want to work with and for. Improving communication doesn't have to be complicated, since small changes in communication can lead to huge benefits. To increase the likelihood that you will continue improving, start small: choose one tip, tool, or technique and start practicing it today.

Focus on small, well-leveraged changes that will result in an "engaging" style of communication.

CHAPTER 2

Choose Your Mindset

Your mindset – the way you view the world, work, people, experiences, and everything else around you – has a tremendous impact on your ability to use engaging communication. Mindset is a simple concept defined by world-renowned Stanford University psychologist Carol Dweck after decades of research on achievement and success.[10]

Essentially, Dweck contends that there are two basic mindsets: "fixed" and "growth," and the mindset we choose can have a profound impact on our behavior and on our success. These mindsets can be summed up as follows:

Traits

- The "fixed" mindset sees traits such as intelligence as "fixed," or set. A fixed mindset leader would believe that some employees are simply smarter than others and that training, education, or other opportunities are unlikely to change their intelligence level substantially. What an incredibly "disengaging" mindset! This leader or professional doesn't believe people can learn or develop, so they withhold opportunities, don't have meaningful conversations about career advancement, and in general treat those who they see as smart and talented in one way (rewarding) and those who they view as less smart and talented in another (withholding). It is very demoralizing to work for a fixed mindset leader if you are looking to have meaningful performance conversations and/or are looking to report to and work with someone who respects you.

- In contrast, the "growth" mindset sees traits like intelligence as something that can be developed. A growth mindset leader believes that through training, education, and other opportunities, people can learn, grow, and develop. This belief can be the foundation for creating employee engagement. Respecting people's ability to grow and develop can be a precursor to meaningful performance conversations, opportunities to work on interesting projects, and other "engaging" behaviors.

Risk and Change

- The fixed mindset sees risk and change as threats. So, naturally, these leaders place a low value on innovation and new ideas. A fixed mindset leader finds it difficult to encourage people to try new things. They also exhibit stagnant behaviors, such as trying to keep doing things they way they've always been done when innovation would be more effective. It is very disengaging to work in a stagnant environment where opportunities to contribute and collaborate don't exist.

- The growth mindset sees risk and change as opportunities to learn. Naturally, these people are less resistant to change. They are more comfortable with a degree of calculated risk because they know that they may learn from the experience. A growth mindset leader encourages people to innovate, try new things, and be open to creative ways of accomplishing goals. This creates an exciting, dynamic, and engaging environment.

Entitlement

- An individual with a fixed mindset can often feel special, entitled, or better than others. This mindset can foster a "my way or the highway" leadership style where this leader believes that they know best because they have a position of power or authority.

- An individual with a growth mindset can feel good about themselves, but not at the expense of others. This mindset can foster a more open leadership style that involves generous praise and a focus on goal achievement rather than trying to look good or better than others.

Criticism

- Criticism and feedback (even if it is positive) can be viewed by the fixed mindset individual as a threat to the core of their existence. Imagine that all of your life you've been told you have a talent for numbers, that you are "smart" that way. (And remember, with a fixed mindset, you are either good with numbers or you're not; you can't really change.) Any data that contradicts this view – such as being told that you've made a mistake – can cause you, the fixed mindset person to question your entire view of yourself. Feedback that isn't consistent with your self-image can be devastating. As a result, fixed mindset people are not open to feedback – it's just too scary. They also rarely offer feedback. Obviously, this doesn't bode well for meaningful performance conversations.

- A growth mindset individual doesn't see feedback or criticism as a threat. Rather, they see feedback as something that fuels their growth and takes some of the pain out of the learning

5

curve. If they receive feedback that is not in alignment with their self-perception, they don't instantly accept or reject the feedback. Rather, they consider the source, the motivation, and the accuracy of the feedback. Then they either reject the feedback as inaccurate or accept it and allow their self-concept to change. Clearly, this means they value feedback and can participate well in meaningful performance conversations.

Failure

- Fixed mindset people often allow failure to define them. "I failed at this task," they may think, "I must be a failure." Failure isn't a form of feedback or a learning experience; it is devastating to them. A fixed mindset leader is, therefore, very critical of failure in others – fostering an environment where fear rules and innovation suffers.

- Growth mindset people don't allow failure to define them. Failure, for them, is another form of feedback they can learn from. It doesn't devastate them; it motivates them. A growth mindset leader is, therefore, tolerant of failure in others as long as they learn from it – fostering an environment where innovation and creativity thrive.

Without question, the growth mindset individual is the kind of individual more likely to practice engaging communication. And the connection between growth mindset leaders and employee engagement is clear. Research reveals that:

- Managers with a growth mindset notice improvement in their employees, whereas those with a fixed mindset do not (because they are stuck in their initial impression).[11]

- Peter Heslin, Don Vandewalle, and Gary Latham showed that employees evaluated their growth mindset managers as providing better coaching for employee development.[12]

Mindset is that it is just that: a mindset. And you can always change your mind. Many people struggle with some fixed mindset tendencies, and, in fact, we aren't always just one mindset or the other. The great news is, research reveals that simply being aware of these mindset differences goes a long way towards fostering a growth mindset. If you sometimes find yourself in a fixed mindset, then making a conscious effort to overcome those limiting beliefs and choosing a growth mindset will assist you tremendously to communicate in a way that enhances employee engagement.

*Human beings,
by changing the inner attitudes of their minds,
can change the out aspects of their lives.*

~ William James

CHAPTER 3

Change "Will this work?" to "How will this work?"

I t is remarkable what an amazing difference this small change can make! When you simply ask "Will this work?" you are asking a yes or no question. It is then far too easy to answer, "Nope – it won't work" and dismiss a potentially useful or valid tool simply because at first glance, it isn't a neat and tidy solution.

As you read this book, ask yourself "How will this work in my organization?" or "How will this work for me?" When you add the "how" to this question, it opens your mind, broadens your vision, and increases the likelihood that what you learn will be applied. You will also see applications that might not be obvious at first, but can be very valuable in the long run.

Savvy communicators will use this change in language to foster employee engagement. One of the key drivers of employee engagement is making people feel their contributions are valued. When discussing new ideas, instead of asking your team or peers "Will this work?" ask them "How will this work?"

Be prepared for innovative and creative answers! Not only will this question help broaden employees' horizons and open their minds, but it creates an atmosphere where innovation and creativity are not only valued but actively sought. You will also find that employees have a greater amount of "buy-in" or engagement with the answers because they have had a part in creating them.

CHAPTER 4

Words Matter!

The Case of "That" vs. "If"

Remarkable communicators understand on a very deep level that words matter. Words are the currency of personal and professional life. They can ignite excitement, commitment, and dedication. It is the words we choose to use that can help people feel valued, appreciated, and motivated to give their best. It is also the words we choose to use that can trigger defensiveness, hostility, and animosity in others.

As a professional, the words you choose to use and the words you choose to lose can make all the difference with respect to employee engagement. Moreover, even small changes in the words you choose to use can make a big difference in how engaged your employees and peers feel.

To use an example, word choice is a lot like duct tape. If you've ever seen a NASCAR race on television or been to the track, you know duct tape is one of the most powerful pieces of equipment a pit crew will utilize. They will put duct tape over the front grill of a vehicle, and they will either remove or add duct tape during the course of a race. Sometimes as little as an inch of duct tape can increase or decrease airflow over the engine, which can increase speed and performance. One inch of duct tape can make the difference between winning and losing. So it is with the words we choose to use or the words we choose to remove from our conversations.

One of the techniques I would encourage you to adopt is to change a phrase you may use regularly and replace it with a more powerful, positive, effective phrase.

We all know it is important to apologize if we have done something wrong, hurtful, or inappropriate. A leader who can apologize helps to instill trust in those they lead. And when employees trust their leaders, they are more likely to be engaged.

Be mindful – the words you choose when making an apology, even the small words, matter. Consider the case of "that" and "if."

I apologize <u>if</u> I was inattentive during our conversation.
vs.
I apologize <u>that</u> I was inattentive during our conversation.

Which would you rather hear? I vote for version #2, "I apologize that I was inattentive."

When you say, "I apologize if I was inattentive," you are not genuinely acknowledging the hurt, pain or trouble that was caused. In fact, it can almost sound like you are accusing them of being hyper-sensitive or over-emotional.

By contrast, when you say, "I apologize that I was inattentive," you are genuinely taking responsibility for your disrespectful behavior and the hurt and pain you caused. You are communicating in an accountable and emotionally mature fashion.

"That" vs. "If"

One communicates respect. The other communicates disrespect and contempt. This is one of a myriad of examples to illustrate how **words matter. Choose yours wisely.**

*Remember not only to say
the right things in the right place,
but far more difficult still,
to leave unsaid the wrong thing
at the tempting moment.*

~ Benjamin Franklin

CHAPTER 5

Practice Assertive Communication

Remarkable communicators and those who wish to enhance employee engagement understand the difference between passive, aggressive, and assertive communication. Moreover, they choose to engage in assertive communication because assertive communication is respectful communication.

We all know the difference between assertiveness, aggressiveness, and passiveness. Passive communication is communication when you don't stand up for your own thoughts, wants, feelings, or desires. For example, passive communicators might say yes when they would like to say no. Passive communicators are often doormats, or can become victims simply because they don't know how to stand up for themselves.

In the workplace, the passive communicator might ignore performance problems and hope they will somehow go away or resolve themselves. They shy away from meaningful, engaging conversations around performance and other career management issues, thus contributing to employee disengagement.

The aggressive communication style, on the other hand, is disrespectful. The aggressive communicator becomes a bully. The aggressive communicator may use foul or colorful language. The aggressive communicator disrespects the other parties involved. They might communicate by getting in someone's face or using a loud presentation style. They might even scream, yell, or pound on the furniture.

In the workplace, the aggressive communicator can be a bully, a person who lashes out, a leader who is volatile and hostile. The aggressive communicator will interrupt, will dominate conversations, will not be open to compromise, and rarely asks open-ended questions. Of course, this disrespectful communication style contributes to employee disengagement because not only is an aggressive communicator not trustworthy (you never know when they will blow), but they are very difficult to get along with. This kind of leadership fails to foster a pleasant working environment — another key driver of employee engagement.

Assertive communication is communication that respects the rights of both parties.

Assertive communicators stand up for their own thoughts, wants, feelings, and desires without becoming bullies, without needing to cram their opinions down someone else's throat. They also maintain their dignity by standing up for what they think, feel, and believe, and they don't become wimps or doormats. They avoid agreeing with other people solely to try and make them happy, which is how a passive communicator might function.

Assertive communication fosters employee engagement because it is clear communication. While we may not always like where we stand with an assertive communicator, at least we will know where we stand. I believe one of the biggest compliments anyone can pay you isn't to tell you that they think you are right or that they agree with you – it's to tell you that they know where they stand with you.

At its essence, assertive communication is the language of respect. And when we respect our employees our colleagues and leaders enough to communicate clearly and candidly with them, we will foster relationships based on trust, not fear (as is the case with aggressive communicators) or people-pleasing (as in case of passive communicators). Assertive communication fosters respect and trust, which are clear drivers of employee engagement.

The challenge for many professionals is that they want to be more assertive, but they lack the skills or the know-how. The communication tools in this book are all assertive communication tools that can pass the litmus test of communication which respects the rights of both parties. By reading and applying the communication tools you are learning in this book, you are well on your way to becoming a more assertive (not aggressive or passive) communicator who creates trusting and respectful relationships.

*The most important single ingredient
in the formula of success
is knowing how to
get along with people."*

~ Theodore Roosevelt

CHAPTER 6

Right vs. Effective

One of the most powerful communication tools, and one that will help you experience remarkable results, is understanding the huge difference between being right and being effective. As human beings, we are relatively hard-wired to want to be right. We like to get in the last word. We like to be able to say, "I told you so." We like to be winners. Some people see communication as a win-lose activity, and if they need to win, then the only way they can make sure they win is to make sure other people lose.

The challenge is when we communicate from a "need to be right" mindset, we run the very real danger of becoming a "my way or the highway" kind of leader. Common sense tells us this type of leader fosters disengagement since a "my way or the highway" leader doesn't listen to the ideas or contributions of others. (Why should they? They assume they already have the "right" answer!) The "my way or the highway" leader isn't focused on fostering good relationships; all they care about is getting the job done their way. And a "my way or the highway" kind of leader rarely has meaningful conversations about performance – except to tell people they are wrong. All of these are classic contributors to disengagement.

You don't have be a leader to pay a high price for consistently focusing on being right rather than being effective. Teammates don't appreciate working with people who are know-it-alls or who are rigid, unbending, and prone to micro-managing. When you decide it is more important to be "right" than effective, you engage in communication that makes you difficult to work with and for.

In contrast, a remarkable communicator who wants to make a positive impact on employee engagement knows there is a difference between being right and being effective. They are often willing to sacrifice their need to be right in order to be more effective. They are willing to subjugate their need to be the "winner" or to get in the last word so they can better achieve their ultimate goal. They are willing to listen, to be flexible, and to abandon the "my way or the highway" approach in order to achieve better results. Those results might include better relationships, increased innovation, more creative solutions to challenges, and enhanced employee engagement.

I know a CEO who is a very direct communicator. He had a meeting of all of his senior level executives, and during the meeting one of them was pitching a proposal. In the middle of her presentation, the CEO said, "Okay, I've got it. Move on." Now, he's a direct communicator and this didn't shock anybody. However, he was a bit brusque, blunt and quick to speak. The senior executive moved on because that's what the CEO asked her to do – despite the request being a bit tactless and maybe even a bit rude.

After a few moments, though, the CEO said, "Excuse me. I apologize. A few moments ago I was rude and too direct. What I meant to say was, you have my buy-in and I'm ready to move to the next phase of this discussion." He was willing to apologize in order to be more effective. This is someone who understood that in this interaction, it was more important to focus on effectiveness rather than on his ego or his need to be "right." So he admitted he was wrong.

The end result? The senior level executive felt her contribution was valued and her leader was open-minded, humble, and, although he was a very direct communicator, he was also an engaging one.

Regardless of your position within your organization, a commitment to focusing on being "effective" rather than on being "right" can make you easier to work with and for. You will be seen as more reasonable, more collaborative, and an all around better team player. This can make a positive impact on employee engagement because people like to work with individuals who are reasonable, collaborative, and team players.

*We have two ears and one mouth
so that we can listen twice as much
as we speak.*

~ Epictetus

CHAPTER 7

Sorry No More!

One of the keys to communicating in a way that can enhance employee engagement is to be willing to admit when you've made a mistake or when you were wrong. This displays to those you lead and to your teammates that you value relationships, have a reasonably open mind, and understand the importance of sacrificing your need to be "right" in order to be effective.

The key to apologizing in a savvy, professional, sophisticated fashion is to use the words "I apologize" as opposed to "I'm sorry." People hear "I'm sorry" so many times in a day that it has lost its professional punch and doesn't come across as sincere. If you genuinely want your apology to resonate, choose the words that matter, and use "apologize." You will be taken more seriously and you also avoid the damage that can be done by "I'm sorry." "I'm sorry" is a rather weak and powerless phrase, and using it too often can negatively impact your credibility and professional image.

A fascinating research project by a group of social scientists investigated how predators, physical predators who prey on other people, pick their victims. They went into our prison system and interviewed recidivistic prisoners, or in other words, repeat offenders. They asked, "How do you choose your victims?" Of course, the results weren't very surprising. Most of these repeat offenders said, "Well, I look for the easy targets, people who seem to be victims, the people who seem like they won't put up much of a fight."

That's a bit of a "no duh," so the social scientists dug deeper. They asked, "What makes you think someone's a victim?" and of course they got the typical answers about body language and the overall sense that someone is weaker.

There were also some surprising results. Many of these repeat offenders said that they used a technique to confirm whether their target was truly weak. They would be in a big box store, a grocery store, or a shopping center where people would have shopping carts, and these predators would intentionally ram or bump into their intended victim's shopping cart. If the first thing out of the intended victim's mouth was "Oh, I'm sorry," it confirmed for these predators that they had picked an easy target, a victim.

Something about the phrase "I'm sorry" makes people think that we are weak, whereas "I apologize" doesn't have that same connotation.

I encourage you to get rid of the phrase "I'm sorry" because it's overused and sends a weak message. Instead, replace it with "I apologize." Another benefit of this simple change is that it increases the likelihood that people will believe you are sincere — an engaging communication skill.

CHAPTER 8

Communicate in the Positive

Without question, one of the most remarkable communication tools for enhancing employee engagement is to communicate in the positive. It stands to reason, if a positive work environment is one of the drivers of employee engagement, positive communication will help build that environment. Most people enjoy being around people who are positive and upbeat. Very few people like to spend time with negativists or wet blankets or people who regularly talk about how bad things are. Essentially, people don't enjoy spending time with the actively disengaged.

Albert Einstein noted that "the most important decision we make is whether we believe we live in a friendly or hostile universe." The key here is the word "decision," or choice. We get to decide whether we will be optimists or pessimists. In other words, we choose whether we view the things that happen to us as evidence that "they are out to get me" (hostile universe) or as opportunities for growth (friendly universe).

If we want to do our part in creating an engaged culture, we'll choose to have a positive, optimistic attitude. Moreover, we'll let this positive attitude come through in our communication. As Einstein said, your choice of attitude is the most important choice you will ever make.

Communicating in the positive is not only about avoiding the overtly negative behaviors of the disengaged. It is about remembering that words matter and about choosing our words wisely.

Here are two examples of how many of us are unwittingly negative and a simple correction to help you go from negative to positive:

- **Change "That's not a bad idea" to "That idea has potential."** We often say, "That's not a bad idea" when we are not ready to fully commit. Unfortunately, it is wishy-washy communication and sends a negative message. By changing your statement to "That has potential" you still convey an unwillingness to fully commit at that moment, yet you avoid the negativity of "That's not a bad idea."

- **Change "I disagree" to "I see it differently."** When I share this powerful change in live workshops, people are almost always taken aback. Their initial thought is almost always that I am encouraging people to be doormats. Not so at all. This is another example of how much words matter.

When you say to someone, "I disagree," you are setting up an "I'm right, you're wrong" type of dichotomy. You are creating a dynamic in which people will almost always become defensive. When you change your phrasing to "I see it differently," you avoid the win-lose dichotomy. Letting someone know that you "see it differently" achieves the same objective as "I disagree" without triggering as much defensiveness. "I see it differently" allows you to express your thoughts and opinions without disregarding the position of others or making them "wrong." If you are looking to open dialogue and to trigger more cooperation and collaboration, shift from the negative to the positive and change "I disagree" to "I see it differently."

These are just a few ways you can change your communication from negative to positive. There will be more examples throughout this book. When you make a concerted effort to make this change to your communication, you are doing your part to create a positive workplace and convey respect to those that you work with and lead. And, as we have noted previously, this positivity has a direct link to employee engagement.

Ask yourself, which of these positive communication tools can I put into practice today? How can I use this notion of communicating in the positive to become an island of excellence? Am I doing my part to enhance employee engagement by communicating in the positive?

*Kind words can be short
and easy to speak,
but their echoes are truly endless.*

~ Mother Teresa

CHAPTER 9

Ditch the "Don't" and Focus on the Desired Behavior

Many professionals spend a lot of time telling people what they don't want them to do or what not to do. They often forget to tell people what they want them to do or what the desired outcome looks like.

Think about that for a moment. You may spend a lot of time telling your employees: "Don't over-complicate this process," "Don't create gaps in the system," "Don't make personal calls during work hours," "Don't text in meetings." When we spend time telling people what we "don't want," we are not being very clear because we haven't told them what to do instead.

We'll tell people "Here's what I don't want you to do," but we forget to tell them what the right thing looks like. If you're in a leadership role, a management role, or a supervisory role, this is of vital importance because so many employees would love to please their leaders. They would love to do what their supervisor, manager, or leader wants them to do – and they would do it, if only they knew what that looked like.

One of the key drivers of engagement is understanding how what you do makes a difference. If you fail to focus on the positive or the desired behavior and spend too much time communicating the "don't," you can make it difficult for employees to understand how their actions affect the organization or know what it takes to be successful. You'll enjoy much better results if you help your employees understand what success looks like. Help them to understand that their talents and skills make a difference by sharing with them what you want them to do.

If you're curious whether you are positive or negative in your communication, looking at your own writing is an easy way to see how addicted you might be to the negative. I would encourage you to take a moment, go back through some of the email messages you've sent over the past few months, and run a search for the words "no," "not," and "don't."

See how many times in your written communication you tell people what not to do and then ask yourself, "If I'm telling them what not to do, am I taking the time to tell them what the right thing looks like?" Remember that if it's coming out in your writing, that means it is most likely coming out in your conversations, too.

So, as opposed to saying to an employee, "Don't be late," tell them, "Please be on time." That's an example of sharing what the desired behavior is as opposed to the undesired behavior. Start focusing on what the right thing looks like and you will be easier to work with and for, people will have a better idea of how what they do makes a difference, and you will be doing your part to foster employee engagement in your sphere of influence.

CHAPTER 10

**Forget
Forgetting**

Here is another quick way to adjust your communication to focus on the positive, not the negative. **Change "don't forget" to "please remember."**

When we use the phrase "don't forget," we run the risk of triggering defensiveness and hostility in others. We may also inadvertently send a message that we don't trust them or that we think they won't remember. Since trust is a key driver of employee engagement, we want to not only encourage others to trust us, but we want to convey our trust in others. By using the phrase "please remember" or "as a reminder," we are using remarkable communication to enhance employee engagement.

We also increase the likelihood they will remember what we tell them.

To explain why this is so, let's start with a test. Right this very moment, focus all your energy and attention on what I am about to ask you to do. Right now, at this moment, do not think of a pink elephant. I repeat, do not think of a pink elephant.

If you are like most people, you now have a pink elephant occupying your brain. Despite me telling you **not** to think of one, you couldn't help yourself. That is because brains don't function in the negative.

When you tell people "don't forget," you actually plant the undesired, as opposed to the desired, behavior in their minds. This increases the chances that they will do the undesired action — in other words, they will forget.

Practice this with yourself. The next time you are laying awake at night and telling yourself, "I don't want to forget my briefcase in the morning," change that to "I will remember my briefcase." Plant the desired behavior, not the undesired behavior.

The next time you are tempted to tell an employee "don't forget," change "don't forget" to "please remember." Not only will you increase the likelihood that they will remember, but by communicating in the positive, not the negative, you convey respect.

CHAPTER 11

Communicating "Power To" vs. "Power Over"

Many leaders, or others with some degree of control at work, struggle with understanding the difference between communicating from a place of "power to" and communicating from a place of "power over."

Communicating from a place of "power over" implies that leaders have power over those they lead. These leaders therefore tend to be the "my way or the highway" type of manager or leader. "Power over" communication is also a remnant of the old "command and control" form of leadership. A leader who communicates from this perspective sees himself or herself as being above those they lead. They believe they have the power to "make" people do as they request, and as a result, their communication often reflects this "command and control" mentality.

A "power over" leader will use phrases such as:

"I want you to..."

"You need to…"

"Don't you know that…"

"Power over" communicators tend to ask closed-ended questions, view feedback as a threat to their authority, and rarely (if ever) admit they are wrong or have made a mistake.

Everything about their communication is designed to reinforce their position of power. They believe they have the right, and even the obligation, to tell employees what to do. They are often micro-managers or control freaks who insist on having things done their way, even when other (sometimes more effective) ways exist. What a recipe for a disengaged team!

Why do people adopt this "power over" approach? I suspect there could be multiple reasons. A new leader or manager often feels insecure and thus can tighten the reins because they are afraid of a mistake. Additionally, many leaders may have been led by a "power over" leader themselves, and may know of no other way because they've never had a counter-example. Others may feel the need to make themselves feel better by making others feel small or insignificant.

Regardless of the origins, "power over" leadership yields distressing results. Employees don't feel valued, and they are more likely to simply "put in their time and collect their dime" than to be genuinely engaged in the work they are doing. Creative solutions to problems are stifled, fear of reprisals leads to a lack of initiative, and employees don't feel respected.

Compare this with the "power to" approach. The "power to" leader recognizes that while they have authority and power, that power isn't really "over people." Their power is to drive projects forward; their power is to achieve goals and objectives.

When one is led by a "power to" leader, one feels more respected as an individual and more connected to the projects and tasks with which they are involved. An employee is therefore far more likely to feel engaged when working with or for a "power to" leader than when with or for a "power over" leader. This is because a "power to" leader prioritizes the team's goals and objectives above egos, the need to be right, or the desire to win.

There is one word that is the calling card of the "power over" leader. If you can eliminate this one word from your communication and replace it with more positive alternatives, you will be making tremendous strides towards becoming a "power to" leader.

The word to eliminate is **"should."** Stop "should-ing" on people. When we say *"you should do this..."* or *"you shouldn't do it that way; you should do it like this..."* then you are using a very disengaging form of communication. Professionals don't appreciate it when others try to "tell them what to do" and deny them their freedom to choose.

When you **"should"** on people it can trigger defensiveness and animosity, and it can even bring out their "Junior High Selves." We have all experienced the "Junior High Self." It's those little voices in our heads that say, "You're not the boss of me. Don't you try to tell me what to do." When we trigger this defensiveness in others, we not only make our jobs more difficult, but we miss an opportunity to use engaging communication.

Consider the power of replacing "you should" phrases with one of these options:

- It would be better if you did it this way...

- The _____ (project, employee handbook, contract) requires you do it this way...

- Our _____ (customer, bottom-line) benefits when you do it this way...

- Please do it this way.

- It would be better (beneficial, cost effective, etc.) if you did it this way...

When you replace "should" phrases with one of these options, you are engaging in respectful communication that allows others their freedom of choice while still making your preference clear. This is "power to" communication.

When I conduct live workshops around the world, this is one of the small changes that resonates with people the most. I would encourage you (notice that "I would encourage" is another good substitute for "should") to stop should-ing. It is a small change that can have a huge impact on your relationships with others.

When we use "power to" language, we are using remarkable communication to help people feel respected and valued, thus enhancing employee engagement.

CHAPTER 12

Ask Open-Ended Questions

The use of open-ended questions is one of the easiest engaging communication tools. Anyone, at any level in an organization, can use this technique.

Open-ended questions are simply those questions that will have more than a "yes or no" response or more than one "right" answer. For example, "Did you get the Jones report done?" is a closed-ended question because there is only one right answer.

"What is the status of the Jones report?" or "What's up with the Jones report?" are open-ended questions that will get the same information, but in a more engaging way.

In addition to being one of the easiest forms of engaging communication, open-ended questions are also one of the most effective. When you ask open-ended questions (and then listen courteously to the answer), you are sending the message that you value another's thoughts, ideas, opinions, and position. Additionally, you are sending a message that you don't have all the answers and are open to their contributions. This is also a key behavior of "power to" leadership.

Asking open-ended questions offers huge benefits! And it's so very simple. While the types of open-ended questions are innumerable, it is helpful to have a handful of standbys, open-ended questions you can use regularly. Here are a few of my favorites: *Coaching up!*

- What are your thoughts on this?

- How do you think this will benefit ___ (the team, our customer, the bottom-line)?

- What challenges can you foresee?

- What opportunities might we be missing?

- How can this be done ___(better, smarter, faster, more efficiently)?

Integrate these, and other open-ended questions, into your regular communication, and not only will you be seen as a more open, approachable, and respectful individual, but you will gain the added benefit of the insight, experiences, thoughts, wisdom, and ideas of others.

Some individuals have a communication style that "waits to be asked." They function under the assumption that if you want their insight or opinion, you will ask for it. They won't volunteer it. And, if you don't ask for it, they assume you are not interested.

This is in direct contrast to people with a communication style in which they volunteer their opinion whether you ask for it or not. These individuals function under the assumption that just because you didn't ask doesn't mean you won't listen.

If you have the style that will share even without being asked, you may face a communication risk: you might assume that if people don't speak up, it's because they don't have anything to say. That's because if you were in the same situation, you wouldn't wait to be asked – you would simply speak up.

Remember that other individuals might need to be asked for their thoughts or opinions in order to feel free to contribute. Don't let their good ideas go unvoiced for lack of asking. Ask open-ended questions and make it safe for your team and colleagues to share their insights with you. This not only increases their engagement, it can increase yours as well.

Here is a word of caution regarding open-ended questions. Beware of asking too many "why" questions or only asking "why" questions to the exclusion of other types.

Don't get me wrong, asking "why" questions can provide great insight, and sometimes we do, indeed, need to know the "why." The challenge is that if we ask too many "why" questions, we run the risk of putting people on the defensive. In these situations, perhaps another type of question would be a better choice. For example, instead of asking a "why" question, you could ask:

- I'm curious, what's the story here?

- Will you bring me up to speed? I'd like to know more about this situation.

- Help me to understand.

I was coaching an executive recently who was struggling with her peers and those she leads. They often perceived her as demanding and maybe even a bit on the bossy side. After some questioning and conversation, we came to the mutual insight that she asks far more "why" questions than any other type of open-ended question. My advice to her was to come up with a list of alternative open-ended questions she could use in the situations she faces. I encouraged her to write them down and to review them often, increasing the chances that she would use them instead of all the "why" questions.

During our coaching call a month later, she related that she had, indeed, made the list and was using the new questions. Her team's responses to her requests for information and details were much more positive and she felt less bossy, less like a "power over" leader and more like a "power to" leader.

I would encourage you to do the same. Create your own list of engaging open-ended questions. Review them regularly and commit to using them to create a culture of engagement within your sphere of influence.

CHAPTER 13

That's Interesting, Tell Me More

I find "That's interesting, tell me more" to be one of the most useful engaging communication tools – hands down. It can be used in so many situations that I am hard-pressed to name them all.

"That's interesting, tell me more" can stimulate conversation or encourage others to share more information. And when we engage in communication that proactively asks for others' opinions, we are using engaging communication.

Here are a few of the myriad situations where "That's interesting, tell me more" can come in oh so handy.

If you are engaged in "managing by wandering around" – the practice of being visible and interacting with those you lead on a regular basis – you might, on occasion, discover one of your team is doing something that looks odd, questionable, or even wrong. Avoid the temptation to put them on the defensive by asking (or barking), "Why are you doing that?" Instead, try "That's interesting, tell me more about what you're doing."

By phrasing it this way, you encourage others to tell you more about their thought process, reasoning, etc. You might discover that they are, indeed, doing something wrong. However, if that is the case, you can correct them without having to first push through the barriers of defensiveness.

You might also discover that while they might not be doing something the way you would do it, they are nonetheless not doing it wrong. At that point, you can make the decision to focus on effectiveness rather than on being right and let them to do the tasks in the way that works best for them.

It's also helpful to remember that it isn't outside the realm of possibility that the way they are doing it or what they are doing is smarter or more efficient than your approach. They may actually be doing it better. And when you resist the urge to ask "why" and instead use a more open question, they will feel more confident in your willingness to explore new ideas and options.

Communicating this willingness is vital because nothing is more confusing than someone who gives good advice but sets a bad example. If you, as a leader, talk the talk about being open to new ideas and innovation, make sure your communication is in alignment with that commitment. If you say you are "open," but your behavior and communication sends another message, that doesn't foster engagement and likely fosters disengagement. Use "That's interesting, tell me more" to communicate that you are open to innovation.

You can also use this powerful technique when you have no idea what someone is talking about. Sometimes we find ourselves in conversations with people whose communication skills are less than stellar. They may ramble, use vague language, or in general have a difficult time expressing themselves.

When communicating with these individuals, it can be very tempting to cut them off, finish their sentences, or even use very disrespectful or condescending communication. Some examples of that would be asking, "What are you talking about?" in an exasperated tone of voice or saying "Huh?" (With its implied insult, "What are you, an idiot?")

Professionals who want to communicate in a respectful fashion can use "That's interesting, tell me more" to help get more information without insulting an unclear communicator.

It can also be used to help someone who clearly has more to say, but seems to be hesitant to express themselves. In this case, "That's interesting, tell me more" is an encourager. It sends the message that you are listening and that you value them enough to proactively engage them in conversation.

It is also a great tool to use when you are blindsided. Sometimes in conversations, and especially in group settings, someone will say something that can catch us completely off guard. We then find ourselves at a loss for words. While we know what they are saying, we are surprised they are saying it at that moment or in front of that group.

Frequently this can cause us to either get defensive or to display insecurity by becoming frazzled and flustered. The next time you are blindsided or caught off guard, use "That's interesting, tell me more" to buy yourself time to gather your thoughts and form a professional response.

Perhaps one of the more interesting applications of this phrase is to interact with people who are less than truthful. Now, I am not suggesting that you work with a bunch of "liar, liar pants on fire" types. However, I have discovered that there is often a fine line between "positive image management" or "putting a positive spin on things" and fibbing or dancing in the grey area of truth.

Most professionals aren't going to engage in bald-faced lies (although some, unfortunately, do). It's not uncommon, however, for our colleagues and peers to, on occasion, stretch the truth, spin the truth, or only tell the version of the truth that makes them look good.

The vast majority of the time, it is a poor choice to accuse a peer or a colleague of lying. "That's interesting, tell me more" provides a more acceptable response to their story. By using this probing technique, you send a message that "you're on to them" without being accusatory or backing them into a corner. This technique allows the person to save face while still learning that stretching the truth doesn't go unnoticed or unremarked upon by you.

"That's interesting, tell me more" not only has numerous applications, but it is a technique that can be tweaked or adjusted to meet the needs of the conversation or situation. Here are a few iterations you may find useful:

- I'm curious, tell me more.

- Help me to understand, tell me more.

- I'm interested, tell me more.

While the words might change slightly, the sentiment is the same. Use the version that works best for you and the conversation you are in.

"That's interesting, tell me more" is a powerful employee engagement tool. If you integrate it into your repertoire, you will be engaging in remarkable communication that will yield all the benefits of an engaged workplace: innovation, profitability, better shareholder returns, and stronger margins.

CHAPTER 14

Does Anyone Have Any Questions?

A nother small communication change that can create an atmosphere more conducive to employee engagement is to stop:

"Does anyone have any questions?"

You might be wondering if you've read this correctly. If you read "Stop – does anyone have any questions?" then you read it correctly. Many professionals have been taught to ask for questions at the end of a presentation or after giving instructions. The risk is that, by only asking at these certain points, you may create resistance or fear. Therefore, you may decrease the chances of people actually asking any questions.

In a group setting, if you ask, "Does anyone have any questions?" participants might be embarrassed to raise their hands because they are afraid they will look stupid or seem as if they weren't listening.

Imagine the difference if you changed your wording to:

"What can I clarify?"

The entire dynamic shifts, doesn't it? Wording your query this way puts the onus or burden of clarity on you, the speaker. Participants are more likely to ask questions because you were "not being clear" than because they were "not listening" or "too stupid to get it the first time."

This is a remarkable communication tool that fosters clear communication, a driver of engagement that will directly impact employees. When people clearly understand directions, expectations, processes, etc., they are not only more likely to get them right, they are more likely to feel energized as opposed to frustrated.

It is human nature to be more committed or to have more buy-in when you have had some sort of influence or say in the process. Creating dialogue by stimulating questions facilitates this buy-in and goes a long way towards enhancing employee engagement.

CHAPTER 15

Like Best/ Next Time

One of the key drivers of employee engagement is meaningful conversation around performance management and/or career advancement. This presents a substantial challenge for many leaders.

Research indicates that most leaders consider performance appraisals and disciplinary conversation the least favorite of their responsibilities. The result is that many leaders put off performance appraisals, only having conversations about performance when it is absolutely necessary. When performance appraisals do take place, they are perfunctory, a routine ticking of the boxes, and not genuinely meaningful.

Leaders also sometimes will ignore performance problems in hopes that they will go away. It seems easier that way, but it denies employees the opportunity to learn, to grow, and to benefit from course correction.

Compounding the problem is the reality that even engaged people often quit when poor performance goes unaddressed. In an interesting research study, 600,000 top performers were asked if they had ever quit a job. And of course, many of them had, indeed, quit a job. The researchers then asked why. The number one answer was that they didn't like their immediate supervisor.

It's clear that people don't leave organizations. They leave leaders.

In an effort to understand this trend more thoroughly, the researchers asked "What was it about your leader that made you quit?" The answers are revealing. The top three reasons good people leave their leaders are:

1. They don't like reporting to a moody boss.

2. They don't like to be micro-managed.

3. They don't appreciate it when poor performance goes unaddressed.

What this means is that to keep employees engaged, performance and disciplinary conversations are a must. Failing to have these conversations will either result in high turnover, or employees will stay but will likely be disengaged, either actively or passively.

While these conversations are rarely easy, they can be made easier with the right communication tools.

One of the most powerful tools to add to your engaging communication repertoire is a technique called "like best/next time." This technique allows you to give clear performance feedback without making a large production out of the process.

The key to successfully using like best/next time is to recognize that it is a language pattern or template that you can use to communicate a desired behavior change. This pattern can be tweaked or adjusted to meet your specific needs.

The first component is the "like best." A "like best" is just that —

something you like best about the employee's behavior in a particular area. For example:

I like best that there is a lot of detail in this report...

I like best that you are here on time...

I like best that you consistently consider the unique needs of each customer before offering a creative solution to their problems...

I like best that you stay on task during meetings...

I like best that you delegated part of this project to one of your team members...

Part of your success with this technique is to bear in mind that it is a pattern, so it is important to change up the words so that people don't feel "techniqued." A few, among many, other options would be:

- I appreciate...

- You did a great job with...

- You exceeded expectations with...

Another key to success with this technique is to make sure that your "like bests" are specific as opposed to general. When we are specific, make it very clear what behavior we like or want them to repeat. Failing to be specific can cause confusion and can be demoralizing. Consider this scenario:

An employee turns in a report with lots of detail that was well organized in tables and charts. You genuinely appreciate the data in the tables and charts.

The employee spent time on the data in the tables and charts. However, they spent even more effort and energy on including excerpts from customer feedback forms. The employee is very proud of their idea of integrating the excerpts.

So, if you say "Great job on the report," it is human nature for them to assume you are complimenting what they are most proud of: the customer excerpts. However, while you like the excerpts, what you really want them to keep doing is including the data in charts and tables.

The next time they turn in a report, then, the employee makes a tremendous effort to provide those customer excerpts. However, they don't organize the data as thoroughly in charts and tables.

You are not only disappointed in their work product, but you are confused because they did such a great job last time.

The employee is confused because they can sense your disappointment or that something isn't quite right. From their perspective, however, they did what you asked them to do. They did what they thought made you say "great job" — they included the customer excerpts.

It is confusion and disappointment all around. All of this could have been avoided if the "like best" had been specific.

There is an old management saying, "What gets rewarded gets repeated." Use that to your advantage. When you point out specifically what you like best, you will be practicing engaging communication by providing meaningful performance feedback. But you are also engaging in clear communication — and both feedback and clear communication are drivers of employee engagement.

The second part of the like best/next time system is the "next time." A "next time" is the additional behavior you would like to see in the future.

This future focus is very important. Many leaders spend a tremendous amount time explaining why what the employee did was wrong or why it was not the best choice. And while it is certainly good leadership to help people understand the "why," too much focus on that and a failure to address the action that is expected now or in the future can be demoralizing and therefore disengaging.

Next times must also be specific. In order to help people learn, it is important to give them clear guidance. Telling an employee specifically what the right thing looks like while avoiding sounding like a micro-manager can be tough. That's why the like best/next time formula is so very helpful. It is brief. It is concise. It can keep you from micro-managing while still being clear.

It is also important to make sure that next times are positive and that you focus on the desired behavior. For example, "Next time, don't be late" is a poor choice of words. While it's future focused and specific, it is also negative. Change that to the desired behavior, "Be on time," and your focus, your next time, becomes positive. Also remember that the word "don't" is a huge red flag. Ditch the don't and you are more likely to focus on the positive.

Successful next times are future focused, specific, and clearly articulate the desired behavior. For example:

- I like best that you put a lot of detail in the report. Next time please organize the data in spreadsheet.

- I like best that you are here on time. Next time please remember to clock in.

- I like best that you consistently consider the unique needs of each customer before offering a creative solution to their problems. Next time, please run them by your supervisor if they cost more than x amount.

- I like best that you stay on task during meetings. Next time, distributing the agenda ahead of time would be best.

- I like best that you delegated part of this project to one of your team members. Next time please make sure that is noted in the project plan you submit.

As with "like best," it is important to change the actual wording to avoid sounding canned. You can experiment with what seems to work for you. Here are some options:

- In the future...

- On the next project...

- The next step is...

- Now...

A professional I know recently used the like best/next time system to correct the performance of an employee who was prone to giving "attitude" whenever she was given feedback. It sounded something like this:

I like best that you submitted this well ahead of the court deadline. Now we need to insert more relevant case law to support the position.

Notice she used "now" as opposed to "next time." It was, however, still future focused. This communication was successful. The employee didn't give attitude and made the requested changes.

The like best/next time system works best in conjunction with the following guidelines:

- Change up the language; keep the pattern. If you constantly use the same words, you will be seen as insincere. For the technique to work, it is important to use different words so that it isn't predictable and phony.

- Be sincere. Sometimes it is difficult to find a "like best" — look hard. Find something you genuinely like. It is amazing what you see when you go looking for something to praise. There is almost always something to sincerely like best.

- Offer like bests on their own; offer them often. Get in the habit of "catching people in the act of doing something right." Share your like bests (using varying language) regularly. Offering this level of praise is, as Stephen Covey so clearly articulates, like making a deposit into the emotional bank accounts of others. When you regularly offer praise, people are less likely to become defensive or shut down when you offer suggestions for improvement "next time."

While this technique is obviously valuable to those in leadership positions, it has other applications as well.

Colleagues can use this technique to request their peers to change their behavior by simply softening the language slightly.

I think it is terrific that you invited the CEO to attend our project planning meeting. It would be appreciated if you could give us all a "heads up" next time.

Thank you for putting such a great slide deck together. Now can we add some of the updated information I gathered?

I like that you are keeping me in the loop on important projects via e-mail. It would be helpful if you could put my address in the "cc" line so that others will know I am not an owner of the project.

Parents can use this with their children. Frequently, parents use too many words to convey a simple message. This can confuse younger children as to what you really want them to do and make older children (teens) feel like you are nagging them, triggering typical teenage "attitude." By using the simple like best/next time language pattern, parents can remain clear and concise.

I like best that you took the trash out without being asked. Next time, do it before the trash collectors come.

I like that you picked out your own outfit. Now let's find shoes.

> *I appreciated the text telling me you were on your way home since it was past your curfew. Next time, plan better and be home on time.*

This pattern is also a great way to de-brief after projects. Once the project is completed, ask yourself (or the team) "What did we like best?" This conversation will reinforce the positive behaviors that led to the project's success. Then ask, "What could we do differently next time?" This allows you and your team to learn from mistakes or to take what you liked best to the next level on a future project.

Savvy communicators will use this template to ask for feedback from their leaders. For example, if they are in the middle of a project, a professional might ask their supervisor, "What do you like best about what my team is doing so far and what would you like us to do differently moving forward?" Sometimes our leaders need help in providing engaging feedback. To provide this support, proactively frame up the question in a way that gets you the most helpful kind of feedback.

This template can even be used to respond to criticism. If your leader or a colleague points out a mistake or error you've made, you can use this template to respond in a professional fashion.

> *Thanks for pointing that out. Here's what I learned and here's what I will do differently next time.*

The like best/next time template allows you to accept the criticism without getting defensive or overly apologetic. Too many professionals sabotage their image and credibility because they over-apologize (sometimes in a dramatic fashion) for their mistakes. Avoid this pitfall by communicating that you are aware of your mistakes and that you learn from them.

Meaningful performance conversations are a key driver of employee engagement, but it is common for leaders to struggle with them. The like best/next time system can make those conversations easier. When employees know what they are doing well and how they can do even better, they are more likely to put effort and energy into the success of their organizations.

Good, the more communicated,
more abundant grows.

~ John Milton

CHAPTER 16

Beware the "But"

As communicators, we sometimes sabotage our success with one tiny word: "but." It's a little, tiny word that can do tremendous damage.

The word "but" is a negator. Consider the following examples:

I love you, but...

I won so much money in Las Vegas last weekend, but...

I want to help you with your garage sale, but...

We all know what's coming after the "but" – bad news. Essentially, the "but" cancels out the positive message that precedes it. This can occur even if we use "but" in conjunction with some of the engaging communication tools in this book. For example:

I like best that you got the report done on time, but...

We all can hear the bad news, right? It is as if the "but" erases the "like best."

I apologize, but...

In this case, the "but" is often a gateway to an excuse that erases the impact of the apology.

Thank you for calling the client, but...

Again, the "but" is a precursor to something negative or critical that can minimize or even erase the positive first part of the message.

Eliminating "but" from your communication as much as possible can greatly improve the effectiveness and positive impact of your communication.

Often people will ask me about using "however" instead of "but." While not as negative as "but," the word "however" still has the same detrimental impact. The best course of action is to simply eliminate the "but" and not replace it with anything.

I like best that you got the report done on time. Next time please include the data from marketing.

If you must use a word to replace "but," try the word "and."

I like best that you got the report done on time and next time please include the data from marketing.

Words matter. The word "but" is a small word that can do tremendous damage. Since you are making an effort to use engaging communication, why not keep all the positive benefits by avoiding "but" as much as possible?

CHAPTER 17

"Are You Open to Some Feedback?"

One of the easiest ways to enhance the effectiveness of feedback and other performance-related conversations is to gain permission from the participant right at the start. By asking for their permission, you are communicating respect, which is a driver of engagement.

The easiest way to do this is with a simple question:

Are you open to some feedback?

The great news is that people rarely, if ever, say no. And you get an opportunity to convey respect before a conversation that might be somewhat critical.

If you simply jump right into feedback or criticism without asking for permission, you run the risk of triggering defensiveness. People might think, "What are you jumping all over me for?" or "Who asked you?"

Even if they don't say those things out loud, that is what the voice in their head is shouting loud and clear.

You also take the chance of coming across as someone who is a "power over" type of individual. By assuming you have the right to criticize, you are assuming power.

Jumping in and giving feedback without permission is especially risky when you are communicating with a colleague or teammate. The voice in their head might shout, "Who died and made you the boss of me?" or "You're not my boss – it's none of your business what I do." Again, most people won't say these things out loud, but these are defensive thoughts.

When people are defensive, they are not open to learning new things. If someone's defenses are up, then even the most spot on, accurate criticism or feedback that is well intended and respectfully delivered can fall on deaf ears.

Since one of the key drivers of employee engagement is respect, be respectful by asking for permission before jumping in with advice, suggestions, criticism, or feedback. Not only will the recipient be less defensive, they will likely have more buy-in to anything you suggest because they are now part of the process. You will be truly communicating with them as opposed to being a bully or a "power over" leader.

CHAPTER 18

Express Appreciation

Several years ago I was conducting a communication workshop for about 100 leaders from different organizations. In the afternoon, we were discussing simple ways leaders could improve their communication and enhance employee engagement. The conversation turned to the value of expressing appreciation.

Obviously, one of the easiest ways to express appreciation is a simple "thank you." The consensus was that thanking those you manage and lead is a small thing that can make a big difference. Everyone was in agreement on this, with one very clear exception.

A gentleman interjected and disdainfully said, "I don't need to tell the people who work for me 'thank you.' That's what they get a paycheck for!" And he was serious.

The group sat in stunned silence and waited for me to respond to this somewhat difficult gentleman. My first thought was, "Well, now I know why you were sent to this workshop." I was even tempted to ask the audience, "Who would want to work for this jerk?" Instead, I very tactfully (at least from my perspective) honored his right to choose what he would and would not do. And then I reminded him of the benefits of a simple expression of appreciation:

- A simple "thank you" costs nothing and is a deposit in the emotional bank account. And you never know when you might need to make a withdrawal.

- While money is a motivator, it is not the strongest motivator for most people. Moreover, money is not a driver of engagement. An engaged employee will often do amazing work regardless of the size of their paycheck because they like the people they work with and for, they are committed to the organization's mission, and they know what they do makes a positive difference.

- What gets rewarded gets repeated. A "thank you" is a very simple reward that increases the likelihood the employee will engage in the desired behavior in the future.

He didn't buy it, however. He was so very rooted in a "power over" mindset that he was blind to what was glaringly obvious to others.

Check your own mindset. Be willing to offer thanks generously. You also don't have to be a manager or supervisor to use this engagement tip. Colleagues who say "thank you" to one another regularly are helping each other recognize what they do makes a positive difference, and making a difference is a key driver of engagement. Moreover, the liberal use of "thank you" contributes to a positive overall work atmosphere.

One of the interesting things about "thank you" is that people often don't notice when we say it. However, they most assuredly notice when we don't. The "power over" leader who attended my workshop and rejected the notion of saying "thank you" regularly is doing more damage by omission than he realizes. And I go back the question his response sparked in my head: "Who wants to work for that jerk?"

Are you the kind of leader others want to work with and for? Are you using the simple tools that will help you become an engaging leader? Expressing appreciation is key to being a personable leader, key to improving employee engagement, and it will make your job easier.

*To keep a lamp burning
we have to keep putting oil in it.*

~ Mother Teresa

CHAPTER 19

Please

I often conduct leadership workshops that last for two days. It's always fascinating to ask what stands out — to discover what really sticks for participants after about 16 hours of instruction, interaction, practical application, skill practice and all the other components of a good workshop. Almost across the board, the answers include the importance of saying "please" and "thank you." Despite other high-level and often sophisticated tools and concepts that we discuss, a simple "please" stands out as a keeper and is a big "aha" for participants.

I believe that the idea of saying "please" in the workplace is such a surprising concept because so many leaders simply forget to practice basic good manners. And this oversight is not because they are rude, not because they don't know they ought to say "please," and not because they don't respect their employees and colleagues, but because they are busy. We are often so caught up in getting the job done, putting out fires, averting disasters, and running from meeting to meeting pushing against deadline after deadline, that we don't take the time to remember the small things.

I also believe some leaders function under the misconception that saying "please" can make you look weak. I've observed that those who struggle with this perception the most are typically "power over" leaders, not "power to" leaders.

Of course, there is a weak way to use "please." If you consistently phrase your expectations to your team in the form of questions such as:

- Could you do this please?

- Would it be possible for you to please...?

- Would you please do...?

You run the risk of looking like you are constantly asking permission rather than offering direction and setting expectations. This can make you look weak as a leader or as a colleague.

Perhaps one of the weakest ways to use "please" is as a stand-alone question. Many leaders will make a statement, but end by saying "please?" in a questioning tone of voice.

- I would like you to attend the meeting – please?

- This file needs your attention – please?

It is very possible to use "please" consistently, practice basic good manners, and convey respect to those you lead and to your colleagues without appearing weak. It is all about the placement of the word.

- Please give this file your attention.

- Please attend the meeting.

- Please fill in the missing data for our client.

- Please take care of the customer on hold.

By placing the "please" at the beginning of the sentence, you are able to avoid the traps that can make you look weak, while still remaining polite.

As with "thank you," people don't always notice when we say "please." They notice when we don't. Take the time to use "please." It is a simple, yet effective way to convey respect. And since feeling respected is a key driver of engagement, this one small word can yield big results.

*Knowledge
is power.*

~ Sir Francis Bacon

CHAPTER 20

The Art of Praising

Saying "thank you," offering "like bests," and giving people a quick "good job" are all short and simple ways to make a positive impact. Sometimes, however, we want that impact to be bigger. When a peer or an employee does something extremely well, you can take the art of praising to its most powerful level by using a simple five-step process.

Step One - Praise Immediately

Praise is most effective when it is given as soon after the praiseworthy behavior as possible. Too many leaders will wait until performance appraisal time to share the positive feedback, or they will hold on to it until the weekly team meeting so that they can praise the employee publicly.

While that is fine — go ahead and praise during a review and definitely share the good news publicly in team meetings — it is important to praise the individual immediately as well. This is the stuff of Psychology

101: the closer in time the reward is to the behavior, the more strongly the two will be linked in a person's brain. You can double dip, or even triple dip, by praising right on the spot, the moment you become aware of the accomplishment, and praising in more formal venues as well.

Step Two - Use People's Names

People like to hear their names, especially when their name is linked to something good like praise. This feeling even has a biological basis: research reveals that whenever we hear our names, it triggers a very tiny burst of endorphins – the happy hormones. So the pleasure people take in hearing their names is very real. Increase the effectiveness of your praise by using the person's name.

It goes without saying that we should make every effort to get people's names right! This is a more common problem than many might suspect, especially in today's culturally diverse workplace. Take the time to learn people's names and discover how to pronounce them correctly. If you are in a leadership position, this is crucial. Can you imagine how it would feel to show up to work everyday and hear your boss call you by the wrong name or mangle your name? It would be very disheartening, and you would interpret it as a sure sign that your boss doesn't care about you as an individual.

Step Three - Be Specific

While the occasional "good job" is a valuable form of praise, you need to be specific in order to take praise to a more beneficial level. Let people know exactly what it is they are doing well. This helps them to know precisely what to do again in the future.

John, you did a great job staying calm with that demanding customer.

Clair, I am impressed by how you negotiated a more favorable rate with our vendor.

Well done, Maggie. You found some great cost saving opportunities.

Step Four - Point Out the Impact

Of all the steps in the praise model, this is the one that has the most positive impact on employee engagement. After telling people specifically what it is that they did well, point out the impact of their action: the benefit or positive results that it had.

John, you did a great job staying calm with that demanding customer. That is the type of thing that keeps our overall customer service ratings high.

Clair, I am impressed by how you negotiated a more favorable rate with our vendor. It genuinely impacts the unit cost and makes us look great as a team.

Well done, Maggie. You found some great cost saving opportunities. That's the kind of thing our CFO is looking for and it impacts bonuses.

While pointing out the impact takes a bit of time and is not as easy as simply saying "good job," it goes a long way towards helping employees understand how their actions can help the organization achieve its goals and objectives. The more you can tie an employee's behavior to those goals, particularly those that are high-profile, the greater an employee's sense of value.

Point out the impact to help your employees, and your colleagues, draw a straight line between what they do and big picture goals and objectives. This is the step of the praise model that many, if not most, professionals overlook, but it is the one that can impact employee engagement the most.

Step 5 - Ask for a Repeat

Use simple, direct language and encourage people to keep up the good work.

I look forward to the same level of detail on the next project.

Keep up the good work.

Doing it again would be great.

It doesn't need to be overblown or complex. It is simply a way of encouraging the other person to continue the behavior. Use language that comes naturally to you.

Excellent job on this report, Tom. The data is well organized and thorough. That is the kind of thing that keeps us out of regulatory hot water. Keep up the good work.

Delivering praise that is sincere and meaningful can enhance employee engagement. Moreover, it is easy to do. While this five-step model takes a bit more time, effort, and energy than simply saying "good job," it is worth it. If you take the time to use it, you will see improved productivity, increased innovation, reduced turnover, improved profitability, and all the other benefits directly associated with engaged employees.

CHAPTER 21

Practice Straight Line Communication

A n engaged employee is very clear about how their activities make a difference in the overall success of the organization. Typically, that clarity is a result of communication with immediate supervisors, attendance at meetings where important issues are discussed, and formal communication.

Even engaged employees, however, face the risk of developing a blind spot. As a leader, you might attend numerous high-level meetings where key organizational goals and objectives are discussed, and you might also be privy to information from high-level sources. For these reasons, you might have an exceedingly clear knowledge of organizational goals and objectives and your team's role in achieving them. Because it is common knowledge to you, it is easy to forget that those you supervise do not know everything that you know. They don't have the same access to information and resources as you do. They may not be as aware as you are of how their actions impact the organization's success.

Part of the responsibility of every leader is to help those they lead recognize that what they do matters. Avoid simply assuming that they know. Instead, use communication that refers to the organization's key objectives. When praising people, link the behavior to the big picture.

So many disengaged employees feel like what they do doesn't matter. You know it does. Help them to discover that.

You will also find that connecting behaviors to organizational goals and objectives can convey the message that you are a "power to" leader. A "power to" leader is interested in the achievement of everyone on the team; a "power over" leader, on the other hand, is often wrapped up in his or her ego, is very vested in the need to be right or to win, and uses their authority to "make" people do what they want them to do.

Whenever the opportunity arises, create awareness and provide information that helps people draw a straight line between what they do and what the organization values.

CHAPTER 22

In Absence of Good Information...

Respect, one of the key drivers of employee engagement, is enhanced when leaders and colleagues alike do their best to keep people informed.

Jett Communication recently conducted a survey revolving around employee engagement and communication. Respondents were asked what their leaders do that helps them feel engaged at work. The vast majority of the responses contained some variation on the idea that "my leader keeps me informed."

Respondents indicated that "keeping people informed" comes in many different guises. Some of the most popular and effective methods are:

- Regular meetings where big picture issues are discussed.

- Face-to-face casual conversation and interactions throughout the week.

- Timely formal communication through e-mail and other channels, as opposed to communications that are last-minute or afterthoughts.

As a leader, ask yourself, how am I doing with respect to keeping people informed? Am I visible or do I spend all my days in my office and in meetings? Am I sending timely formal communication?

This type of communication is even more important during times of change or upheaval. Instead of simply instigating changes and informing people about the "how" of the change, respect your employees and your colleagues enough to share the "why."

Let people know why the changes are necessary or wise. Allow them access to the data, information, or details that drove the decision, and describe the rationale used to make it. While people might not take advantage of this transparency, they will still feel respected because you gave them the opportunity to know the information.

Failure to keep people informed and to tell them "why," on the other hand, fuels active disengagement. It may also potentially be the tipping point for those who are on the verge of crossing over into the actively disengaged camp.

As you may recall, actively disengaged individuals are those who overtly display their disenchantment. They gossip, are very resistant to change, and spread negativity among other destructive behaviors. Now remember that in the absence of good information, people will make things up! Rumors start in information vacuums and end up as weapons in the hands of the actively disengaged.

Trust your employees enough, even enough to give them the bad news, and they will often trust you in return. Keeping people informed is a sign of trust and a form of engaging communication.

CHAPTER 23

A Few Habits to Break

Even the most conscientious professional can have a few bad communication habits. It's possible, then, for a leader who is committed to enhancing employee engagement through remarkable communication to sabotage their own success. They can unwittingly shoot themselves in the foot. Here are a handful of habits to break – now!

1. Stop beginning with "honestly" or "to be honest with you."

While most people recognize that you are not lying all the other times you speak, overusing "honestly" or "to be honest" is an annoying habit that many people are hyper-sensitive to.

Your use of the word may signal that you are going to communicate in a very direct or candid fashion, and it may be an attempt to soften your direct communication. The problem is that it doesn't typically soften the message in an effective fashion, and it can annoy your listener. Moreover, it can send a message that you don't trust your employees, colleagues, and/or peers to handle the truth. It is insulting and disengaging to start with "honestly." Purge "honestly" or "to be honest with you" from your conversations.

2. Stop using "don't take this personally" or "no offense."

All this does is communicate to your listener that you are about to say something hurtful and you want to shift the responsibility for that hurt from you to them.

It's almost as we are looking for a "free pass" to say mean or disrespectful things simply because we first tell the listener not to be hurt or upset. And, when they inevitably do become hurt or upset, we often attempt to make it their fault by saying something like "I told you not to be upset." (Translation: "I warned you — it's your own fault you were hurt.") This is a very passive-aggressive form of communication.

The next time you are tempted to say "don't take this personally" or "no offense," stop and ask yourself "Is this really necessary to say?" or "What am I trying to accomplish — do I want to be hurtful or helpful?" When we are tempted to use these passive-aggressive phrases, let it be a signal to us that what we are about to say is best left unsaid or said in a different way.

3. Stop using disclaimers such as "I might be wrong" or "I might be the only one who thinks this."

Confident communicators don't weaken their message with disclaimers. If you start out by saying "I might be wrong," a listener might agree with you and close off to you. Or since you essentially gave them tip-off, they might spend their time looking for ways you might be wrong. Many listeners will also wonder, "If you are not confident, why are you wasting my (our) time by speaking?"

Other popular disclaimers are "This might be a dumb question" and "This might not work, but..." When we use such disclaimers, we sabotage our credibility and lessen our message's impact. Purge disclaimers from your communication. People want to work with and for others who are confident, and they are more engaged when they have confidence in their leaders. Beware the self-sabotage of this habit.

4. Stop playing the blame game.

No one likes to report to or work with someone who doesn't take responsibility for their own actions. And they may absolutely dread reporting to or working with someone who blames others. Such a person communicates that nothing is ever their fault or their responsibility.

The research is very clear that blaming others – other teams, other departments, organizational policies, the budget, the economy, the lay-offs, etc. – is a sign of someone actively disengaged. If you are reading this book, it is highly likely that you are skilled at avoiding the overt blame game. Many professionals, however, have a communication habit that is a subtle form of it. Stop using phrases such as:

- He made me so angry!

- She makes me so frustrated.

- You make me sad.

The common denominator is the word "make." Phrasing emotions this way can make you look like someone who blames others and considers themselves a victim. There is a simple change that will keep you out of the "blame game" altogether.

Change "you make" to "I am."

- I am angry.

- I am frustrated.

- I am sad.

"I am" statements allow you to take ownership of your state as opposed to blaming someone else. They allow you to clearly express your feelings without needing the safety net of blaming others. "I am" language is accountable language.

Choose to use the language of accountability and you will set a good example for those around you, be seen as a more confident and responsible leader, and won't be viewed as a conduit of negativity.

According to recent research conducted by Jett Communication, people often think they are behaving less negatively in the workplace than their peers think they are. Engaging in the "blame game" is the type of inadvertent negative communication that often explains this difference in perception.

Pay attention to how you phrase things as a leader and avoid "you make" language. Break this bad habit today.

5. Stop saying "I don't care."

"I don't care" or "I don't mind" – is there a difference? Since words matter, I believe there is a difference. If you are a leader looking to use communication to improve employee engagement or a professional working to foster great working relationships, you will carefully consider the words you choose to use and the words you choose to lose. "I don't care" is a phrase to lose.

When you say "I don't care" in response to a casual question or request, you run the unintentional risk of conveying that you genuinely DON'T CARE – and that is likely a message you want to avoid. No one wants to work with or for people who don't care. No leader can bring the best version of themselves to work everyday if they don't care. When we say we don't care, there is a chance that people will believe us.

So, what do we say instead? Here are some options that don't risk unintentionally sending a "disengaging" message and also probably express your thoughts more accurately:

"I don't mind" or "that's fine"

"I don't have a preference" or "whichever you prefer"

This is a small change that can make a big difference in how you're perceived and the message you send.

6. Stop the "just" and "little."

Few things can be as demoralizing as having someone belittle or demean something you believe is important or valuable. And yet, that is what many of us inadvertently do when we choose to use the word "just" or "little."

"Just" and "little" are minimizers. They make whatever you are describing seem small or less than it might be.

- *"I just need a moment of your time."* This can inadvertently convey that either what you are about to ask them to do isn't very important or that you don't value their time.

- *"We have a little problem."* This may convey the literal meaning: the problem is small or little. The consequence of this is that people might not pay much attention to the issue or problem. They might not give it their best effort or they may not prioritize it highly. Alternatively, they might believe that you are bringing them this small problem because small problems are the only ones you consider them capable of handling. Tasking people only with "little" problems might inadvertently send the message that you don't trust them with anything significant.

- *"You just need to..."* The word "just" in particular can send the message that the solution to their challenge or situation is very simple or easy, potentially ignoring the complexity or seriousness of the issue. You create the impression that you have all the answers and that the solution is obvious. This can be insulting.

Using the minimizers "just" and "little" can devalue people and their contributions. Monitor your communication with those you lead and with your peers. Are you sending a demeaning message? Engaging communicators help people feel valued, not devalued. Stop the "just" and "little."

▌CHAPTER 24

Information absorbed is knowledge.
Knowledge applied is wisdom. It's not what you know that matters.
It's what you do with what you know.

This book is jam-packed with remarkable communication tools and techniques you can use to enhance employee engagement, regardless of your position in the organization. At the beginning of this book you were encouraged to keep in mind:

How will this work for me?

So, how will it work for you? What specific changes are you going to make in your communication? How are you going to choose to be an island of excellence?

Here are a handful of questions designed to help you convert your knowledge into action.

- What three small communication changes in will I make in order to make a big difference?

- What three words/phrases will I stop using, and what will I use instead?

- What tool will make the biggest difference in my organization?

- We learn best when we teach others. What insight have I gleaned that I can share with my leader? With my colleagues? With those I supervise?

Around the world, employee engagement is in a downward trend. Organizations are suffering the negative impact of the actively disengaged and losing the opportunity cost of the passively disengaged.

While there is no quick fix or band-aid that will make everything better, focusing on communication can have a broad, sweeping impact across all organizational boundaries. Improving your ability to practice engaging communication is one thing you can do to make a positive difference.

Remember, it's a lot like duct tape and NASCAR racing: small adjustments can have a huge impact. Commit to making your small changes today!

ENDNOTES

1   Kenexa (2011/2012). *Engagement Levels in Global Decline: Organizations Losing a Competitive Advantage*, a 2011/2012 Kenexa High Performance Institute Worktrends Report

2   Gallup

3   Towers Perrin (2011). Towers Perrin Global Workforce Study

4   Kenexa (2011/2012). *Engagement Levels in Global Decline: Organizations Losing a Competitive Advantage*, a 2011/2012 Kenexa High Performance Institute Worktrends Report

5   Towers Perrin (2011). Towers Perrin Global Workforce Study

6   Gallup

7   Kenexa (2011/2012). *Engagement Levels in Global Decline: Organizations Losing a Competitive Advantage*, a 2111/2012 Kenexa High Performance Institute Worktrends Report

8   Towers Perrin (2011). Towers Perrin Global Workforce Study

9   Tom Peters and Robert Waterman (2004.) *In Search of Excellence: Lessons from America's Best-Run Companies*

10 Carol Dweck (2007). *Mindset: The New Psychology of Success*

11 Peter A. Heslin and Gary P. Latham, *The Effect of Implicit Person Theory on Performance Appraisals*, Journal of Applied Psychology, Vol. 90, 2008

12 Peter A. Heslin, Don Vandewalle and Gary P. Latham, *Keen to Help? Managers' Implicit Person Theories and Their Subsequent Employee Coaching*, Personnel Psychology, ABI/INFORM, Winter 2006

Take the 5-Minute Survey on Employee Engagement and Communication Today!

When you do, you will receive a complimentary download of one of Pamela's most popular teleseminars - *a $79 value!*

Simply visit:
www.surveymonkey.com/s/engaging-communication

ABOUT PAMELA JETT

For more than twenty years, Pamela Jett has been helping professionals develop remarkable communication skills for remarkable results. With a passion for helping professionals accelerate their careers, build better relationships, and experience greater productivity, she has developed language patterns, workable communication templates, and guidelines to help people succeed in even the most challenging communication situations. Now she is putting her communication expertise to work helping to address the global crisis of employee engagement.

With a distinguished, worldwide clientele that includes Fortune 500 companies, C-suite executives, and a multitude of associations and organizations, Pamela brings her innovative tools to life through keynote presentations, training, and coaching. Her style is engaging, energetic, and down-to-earth.

In addition to possessing an impressive academic vitae that includes time as a university professor, Pamela has been honored with the CSP (Certified Speaking Professional) designation from the National Speakers Association and currently serves in a variety of volunteer leadership positions within that organization.

When not speaking, training, or coaching, she lives in Mesa, Ariz. (it's a dry heat!). Her passion for travel, learning, and speaking is only surpassed by her love of a great novel and laughing as often as possible.

Additional Resources
by Pamela Jett

These powerful programs and many others are available on-line at JettCT.com/success-store

What to Say? 7 Secrets of Remarkable Communication Techniques that Produce Remarkable Results

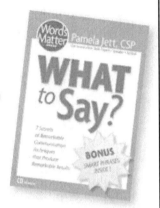

It is no secret - communication is your most important skill. In this powerful audio CD program, Pamela Jett, CSP, shares 7 secrets of remarkable communication for remarkable results so that you can more confidently know what to say even during some of your most difficult conversations.

Mind Your Own Business: A Career Management System

It's a myth that "good work gets noticed." To receive attention, authority and in organizations you must manage your own career success. In this fast-paced and entertaining program you will learn to develop a strategy to "mind your own business" and succeed.

www.marketerschoice.com/SecureCart/SecureCart.aspx?mid=30C38C41-84DC-4E90-97E2-5AA94E6BB532&pid=7af211769e2f9f98f076e7b3b95b565b

Communicate With Confidence, Credibility and Influence

A Woman's Guide to Becoming a More Powerful, Effective & Persuasive Communicator *(6 Disc Audio CD Set)*

As a professional woman, you want others to see you as a strong, competent, take-charge individual. Discover effective communication tips on how to master confident communication to achieve the powerful position you desire.

Success is an Attitude

Master the Right Attitude and Remove Roadblocks to Success

All great success in life starts out with one fundamental—the right attitude! Everyone in your organization can benefit from this program and discover how to efficiently manage their attitudes.

Looking to share what you've learned?
Call 866.726.5388 and ask about bulk order discounts!

Connect With Pamela Jett

 **Pamela Jett**

Pamela Jett, CSP

Pamela Jett

PamelaMJett

Pamela Jett
Jett Communication Training, Inc.
P.O. Box 7385
Mesa, AZ 85216

866.726.5388

JettCT.com

info@JettCT.com